A Director's Guide

Innovation

THE KEY TO COMPETITIVE ADVANTAGE

Editor, Director Publications: Tom Nash
Managing Editor: Lesley Shutte
Production Manager: Victoria Davies
Design: Halo Design
Commercial Director: Simon Seward
Managing Director: Andrew Main Wilson
Chairman: George Cox

Published for the Institute of Directors
and 3M
by Director Publications Ltd
116 Pall Mall London SW1Y 5ED

Editorial: 020 7766 8910
Production: 020 7766 8960
Sponsorship: 020 7766 8885
Copy sales: 020 7766 8766
Facsimile: 020 7766 8990

YOURS TO HAVE AND TO HOLD
BUT NOT TO COPY

Director Publications Ltd
116 Pall Mall
London SW1Y 5ED

Kogan Page Ltd
120 Pentonville Road
London N1 9JN

©Director Publications Ltd 2000

British Library Cataloguing in Publication Data
A CIP record for this book is available from the British Library
ISBN 0 7494 3423 6

Printed and bound in Great Britain

Contents

1 An accident happens in an instant.

2 It's comforting to know that 3M is there.

Cuts and scrapes are bad enough, without having to contend with uncomfortable dressings that don't stay put on elbows, knees, fingers or knuckles. 3M combined our unique non-woven material with a gentle adhesive to create a dressing that's so soft and comfortable, you'll hardly know it's on. 3M™ Nexcare™ Comfort Strips stretch and flex the way you do, staying where you put them until their job is done. The whole family will appreciate the benefits of Comfort Strips. They're just one more product developed from our unique corporate culture in which life's little bumps provide the inspiration that enables us to make the leap

from need to...

3M *Innovation*

Innovation is a never-ending commitment

George Cox, Director General, Institute of Directors

The concept of innovation is often associated with the single big, new idea: the dramatic one-off breakthrough. However, in today's world, innovation has to mean more than this. It has to become a continuous way of life. Only those companies that recognise this, and are equipped to deal with it, are going to succeed.

Of course, short-term success can be achieved with a bright idea: the super new product or the imaginative new internet service. Such opportunities have never been greater. However, the one big innovation that has got a company into the game - even if it has made a financial killing - is only the entry ticket. The circumstances that brought about the initial success have to be turned into a lasting feature.

Long-term success requires a change to the fundamental nature of the business. After all, innovation is not only about creating new and better products and services. It also means identifying and forging links with other organisations, to secure funding or tap into special expertise or knowledge. Equally important is the safeguarding of intellectual capital and business profits through the proper use of IP law.

Today's companies must be able to respond quickly to market opportunities, new competitive threats or changed economic circumstances. To do this companies need to nurture and maintain an open culture, where teamworking and the sharing of ideas - at all levels - are actively encouraged. Sustainable innovation will be the key to future success for every business.

1 We've been on a roll for 67 years.

2 Now we've popped up with another big idea.

It's an ingenious dispensing system that pops up strips of tape – pre-cut, one

at a time, right into your hand. New Scotch® Tape Strips make

everyday taping tasks easier, especially when

you've got your hands full.

We're making tape even more handy,

because we make the leap

from need to...

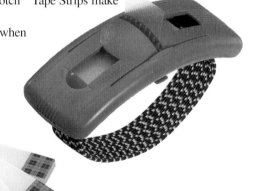

3M *Innovation*

For more information, call 08705 360036, or Web site: http://www.3M.com/uk

Competing through innovation

Livio D DeSimone, Chief Executive Officer, 3M

Innovation has been a core concept at 3M for decades, and a central element of our vision: "to be the most innovative enterprise and the preferred supplier." We believe strongly that a culture of innovation offers a company a number of unique strategic and competitive advantages, which are increasingly important in today's fast-moving and competitive marketplace.

First, innovation provides a self-renewing means to satisfy customers. Second, it can help establish and increase one's market leadership. In head-to-head battle, the innovator has a greater opportunity to establish clear advantage and differentiation over competitors. Third, innovation provides a powerful engine for growth. New ideas and solutions lead to new product categories and new markets. And, by providing a steady stream of new solutions, growth through innovation can serve to attenuate the fluctuations of economic cycles. Finally, our experience has been that innovation is a supreme motivator of people, a source of challenge and excitement for our employees. It unleashes creativity – both in the organisation and, more importantly, in the individual.

We have learnt that innovation is not for the fainthearted. The freedom to innovate brings a measure of chaos. There is a definite element of disruption, but the benefits are extraordinary.

3M's corporate culture is the result of conscious attention and hard work by many people over many years. And sustaining our culture will require conscious attention and hard work for years to come. At 3M, innovation helps to determine our future by helping us create our own future.

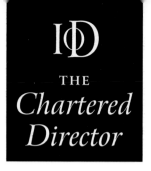

THE
Chartered Director

Be recognised as a professional director

CHARTERED DIRECTOR

The IoD's Chartered Director initiative ensures directors' continued professional education and development.

CRITERIA

Admission to the profession of Chartered Director is open to all IoD members and Fellows with the requisite qualifications who are able to demonstrate the knowledge and experience required to become a member of the profession and who undertake to observe the IoD's Code of Professional Conduct.

BENEFITS

There are clear personal benefits to becoming a Chartered Director. They are recognised as directors:

- *who have achieved standards of professional knowledge and experience;*
- *who have made a serious commitment to their profession;*
- *who have undertaken to act with probity and honesty.*

The letters *C.Dir* that Chartered Directors may append to their names are an easily recognisable badge of professionalism.

As a condition of continued registration, "chartered" members must commit to Continuing Professional Development (CPD) – at least 30 hours a year keeping themselves abreast of both practical and theoretical developments in direction.

To find out more about becoming a Chartered Director, telephone 020 7451 3210, or visit the IoD's web site at www.iod.co.uk

The IoD is ideally suited to help Chartered Directors achieve their Continuing Professional Development (CPD) requirement.

Look out for this symbol which is displayed on IoD products and publications that can assist directors in achieving their CPD requirement.

Chapter 1

Creating the right climate for innovation

What is the impact of innovation on the UK economy, and how do we compare with our foreign competitors? Roger Trapp, management writer for the Independent, investigates

Today's companies feel they have to be innovative, perhaps even more than they believe they have to be global. This is largely a response to the fundamental shake-up in the industrial landscape being created by the internet and its various spin-offs, but is also a recognition that the cost-cutting with which much of Anglo-Saxon business was obsessed in the late 1980s and 1990s cannot by itself produce sustainable success.

Professor Gary Hamel, the strategy guru, has been particularly vocal in warning that at a time of low inflation – like the present – the only way for companies to grow is to innovate, by launching new products, improving service and conducting their business in different ways.

This message has been reinforced by some management consultancies, which regularly publish surveys demonstrating the importance of coming up with new ideas and implementing them. And yet, for all this attention and approval, innovation appears to remain a fringe activity among UK companies.

The UK has a handful of individual heroes – such as James Dyson, inventor of the new form of vacuum cleaner; speed ace Richard Noble; and Trevor Baylis, of clockwork radio fame. And there are certain sectors – notably pharmaceuticals, supermarket retailing and telecommunications – that are rightly commended for their ability to come up with new products, services and approaches.

A recent report by management consultancy Booz-Allen & Hamilton pointed out how British companies were doing better in this respect than many of their continental European counter-parts. Yet much of the country's industry seems to be stuck in the "me-too" trap, where the only differentiator is price.

FALLING BEHIND ON RESEARCH AND DEVELOPMENT

Research and development expenditure is one of the most obvious measures of commitment to innovation – and here Britain does not fare too well. According to the latest R&D Scoreboard, published by the Department of Trade and Industry's Innovation Unit in June 1999, the UK's biggest companies spent more in the previous 12 months than they had in any of the three years leading up to that period. Even then, they were still far short of international levels. While the world's 300 largest companies spent five per cent of their sales on R&D, companies in the FTSE 100 spent just 2.1 per cent, or less than half that proportion of turnover. Among those in the next tier down, the so-called mid-market 250 companies, the figure was only 1.3 per cent.

However, the picture is slightly confusing. As the DTI points out: "...some of the difference seen in the Scoreboard between the overall British and international levels of R&D investment can be attributed to the mix of companies in the UK". In other words, many of the largest UK companies are not in sectors where heavy R&D investment as a proportion of sales is vital to success. Even so, the results were enough to cause government ministers to question why a significant proportion of UK companies appear to place less emphasis on R&D than their international competitors.

The Innovation Unit did little to lift the gloom when, six months later, it published its latest assessment of how much British companies were spending on tangible assets, such as plant and machinery. The Capital Expenditure Scoreboard was introduced because this activity is seen as essential to companies' profitable growth. The second annual report, published in December 1999, showed that British companies as a whole last year invested £10,000 in plant and equipment for each person they employed, compared with £15,200 by their leading international competitors.

Again, the picture is a little confusing. Some of the sectors in which Britain excels – including supermarkets and telecommunications, where companies such as Tesco and Vodafone are world leaders – saw significant levels of capital expenditure. Meanwhile traditional big spenders such as engineering companies lagged behind. But, overall, the findings showed that British companies were spending enough to avoid falling further behind international competitors, but not enough to catch up.

BLIND MAN'S BLUFF

So, why is it that so much of industry fails to see what is so obvious to so many and not spend the money they need to grow? It is tempting to blame the government for continuing to burden growing businesses with regulations and for not doing enough to foster a risk-taking culture where failure is tolerated. But the UK has enjoyed economic stability for some time and low tax rates together with various investment incentives are helping to create an environment that is reasonably benign if not actually helpful.

What is more, in applauding the likes of Bill Gates – for developing ideas that have given Microsoft a market worth far in excess of the value of its tangible assets – the UK government is seeking to demonstrate its intention to embrace the new economy and encourage British industry to play a full part in it.

As for the City, it is traditionally criticised for being overly short-termist. Yet analysts insist that they generally put a positive view on such spending, on the grounds that, if made wisely, these investments produce greater returns in the future.

Greater understanding among government officials and those involved in the stock market would help. Similarly, forms of learning that develop creative ability need to be introduced to the education system and measures taken to halt the trend of talented scientists and other "innovators" to head for the more attractive environment of the US.

LOOKING BEYOND THE QUICK FIX

At the same time business has to help itself. One particular challenge is the need to overcome what Gary Hamel terms "an addiction" to cutting costs and shedding jobs. But, perhaps even more important is the need to break out of the obsession with the quick fix. To be fair, companies have been encouraged to think that such solutions exist through management consultancies and specialist organisations advising on new product development and ways to stimulate creativity and innovation.

As a "bolt-on" extra, called into play when the management is desperate for a new idea or needs a new product quickly, initiatives such as brainstorming and de Bono-style creative thinking sessions have little long-term effect. As John Buckley, head of the technology group in PA Consulting, stresses, large organisations, in particular, are more inclined to kill off ideas than encourage them because of the risks. Similarly, installing intranets and other sophisticated forms of information technology with a view to managing and sharing knowledge will only go part of the way. As the new economy develops, it is becoming increasingly clear that people and culture are going to have the most important role.

PricewaterhouseCoopers, the international management consultancy, said in its latest review of innovation around the world, published last December, that "the most valuable organisations of tomorrow will be idea-rich, have a culture where innovation is embedded as a core capability and value, and will embrace new and unusual ways of fostering innovation".

One of the examples given by the firm of new ways to innovate is the creative use of external and internal venture capital, which it refers to as a "fillip to innovation". As part of this, it is vital that organisations realise that they should not seek to do everything for themselves. Companies can be innovative by using corporate venturing and other approaches to forge links with organisations that offer special expertise or knowledge. This is commonplace in biotechnology and telecommunications, where small start-ups might achieve impressive results with the support of larger organisations that do not otherwise have access to such fresh thinking.

Even more important is the growing emphasis on having an open management style where ideas are encouraged to bubble up everywhere, rather than being confined to R&D or new-product teams. Sean Blair helped develop this thinking into the concept behind "the new business of design" while director of design and communication at the Design Council.

Now, as one of the founders of the consultancy Limited Nowhere, he is going further. He believes that innovation is a practice, not a process, and argues that, to be truly successful, a company has to have innovation at its heart.

CUSTOMERS, CULTURE AND COURAGE

But companies also need to look outwards. Just as all employees have a vital role in producing new ideas, so, too, do customers.

In the end, it comes down to culture, management and leadership. Senior executives must continually remind all employees of the importance attached to innovation and the attitudes and ways of behaving that encourage it. They must also emphasise that – in the information age especially – being innovative in the past is no guarantee of having the answers in the future. Innovation is a continuous process that must constantly be reinforced.

Perhaps this is why Hewlett-Packard, the electronics company noted for its commitment to innovation, has recently launched a marketing campaign reminding its customers, but also its employees, of its origins as a start-up.

Chapter 2

At the sharp end

Innovation has long been at the very heart of 3M's growth and development. William E Coyne, the company's senior vice president for research and development, assesses the impact it has had on the company's success

Innovation is a strange thing. On one hand, it embraces the new and surprising. On the other hand, it occurs in a world marked by accelerated change. And the unpredictability of this world calls for discipline and structure for successful implementation.

Both unpredictability and order are essential for innovation. But too much of either can result in failure, so the trick is to find the right balance. This is not a simple task and a little bit of luck is always liable to be part of the equation.

Innovation, however, cannot be turned on and off like a tap. The only way to achieve sustainable bottom-line improvement is through top-line growth, and the best way to achieve that is through a constant flow of innovative, new differentiated products and services. For this to happen, however, many companies need to adopt new management styles and spend less time plotting strategies to hit predetermined objectives. More time should be spent on guiding the sometimes passionate, sometimes curious, actions of highly innovative individuals. In short, they need to develop a different kind of corporate culture.

DEVELOPING A STRATEGIC VIEW

Innovation is critical to 3M's enterprise and we challenge ourselves to excel at it. We don't just mean in the lab either, innovation is everyone's job at 3M, and it is a job that's never finished.

Innovation has become part of our brand promise. When a customer buys something from 3M, they know they buy a product that incorporates the latest and most sophisticated technology, whether it is a piece of sandpaper, a fibre optic connecting system or a CFC-free asthma inhaler.

We also stimulate and invest in innovation. Our goal is to derive 30 per cent of our sales from products introduced in the past four years. But to turn on the heat, 3M recently introduced a new goal: that 10 per cent of sales must come from products launched in the past 12 months. We achieved both these targets last year.

To sustain the flow of new products, we continue to invest about $1bn a year in R&D, and as a manufacturer we are particularly proud of our patent portfolio growth. During 1998, we were awarded 611 US patents, placing us 10th among US companies. In 1999, 517 US patents were awarded to 3M.

There are times when we challenge the current thinking on innovation. In *The 3M Way to Innovation*, Gundling Ernest proposes the following business model:

- *Managers analyse technological and market trends and select an industry that presents attractive opportunities;*

- *Managers then target part of that industry – a market segment or product line – based on the risk ratio, the company's current presence in the market and other factors;*

- *Finally, the managers determine the technologies and other resources that are required to compete. These resources are acquired and applied.*

While we believe in strategic planning, we've begun to look at product development in a new light. We have learnt that our greatest success comes from developing those products our customers haven't thought of yet, such as the Post-it Note.

We still listen intently to what our customers would like to change in existing products, from increased performance to better environmental characteristics. But we can see no advantage in limiting the number of ideas we are exposed to. As a consequence, we also search for unarticulated needs, solutions to problems our customers have become resigned to or don't even know they have.

TECHNOLOGY TRANSFER

The company draws on a rich pool of over 100 technologies. Thirty of these constitute technology platforms that produce a family of products for multiple markets. While a division must define products and generate sales, no business has proprietary control of a technology which must be shared across the company.

Another approach to product innovation is to start with a company's unique resources that a competitor would find hard to imitate. Here, the same questions are addressed but in reverse order and, unlike the earlier business model, this approach generates unique, proprietary, high-margin products.

As an illustration, take the recent explosive growth in the electronics industry. 3M could have purchased the technology and equipment, hired the personnel and jumped right into one attractive area, such as semiconductors.

Many other companies following the same model would have done so. But we opted for a different route. Over the years we realised that some of our proprietary technologies could be applied to make flexible circuits in an innovative roll-to-roll process. This approach called for close liaison with customers and because the products are based on 3M technologies, we faced little competition. Today, the product has changed the basis of competition in our new and existing markets and offers enormous sales and profit potential. Moreover, it gives our customers a significant edge over their competitors.

Technology is vital for innovation but it is only one step in the process. Someone, somewhere has to come up with a bright idea and that idea, in turn, must be commercialised into tomorrow's products and services.

BUILDING A TRADITION OF INNOVATION

Today, it is widely acknowledged that the greatest challenge for management is to create the right conditions for innovation to flourish. Sadly there is no magic recipe for successful innovation. Individual companies have to learn what to do for themselves. We are still learning almost a century later. But it is this deeply ingrained and dynamic culture, built through the boom years and the recessions, that is 3M's greatest resource and our most immeasurable asset.

Innovation may delight customers but we should not forget the enormous satisfaction it generates for the people who create it in the first instance. At 3M, our teams and divisions operate with a great deal of autonomy. We believe this stimulates freedom and accountability. For this reason, we believe innovation can work in every organisation, regardless of size or industry.

In addition to the company structure, we have a culture that stresses communication and the sharing of discoveries. Many of our innovations are the direct result of cross-functional activities. Other successful products result from collaborative partnerships outside the company with creative customers.

Individual empowerment is important too and we give people time to follow their muse. An unwritten rule permits all technical employees to devote 15 per cent of their time to a project of their own invention. In reality, some use more time, others less – what is important is that the system has some slack in it.

For this to work, the scientist and the company must understand that innovation involves a high degree of failure. Approximately 90 per cent of the ideas put forward by our researchers fail at one of the various "gateposts" before reaching the status of a formal project. The key is to spot the losers early and reduce both financial and organisational risk.

Finally, we've learned that there is nothing more rewarding than recognition from your peers. We are fortunate to have many talented innovation "champions" at 3M who share best practice across the global community and create the fertile ground that often spurs the development of future innovative products or ongoing improvements of existing ones. One of our innovation "champions", Mr William L McKnight, penned a statement around 1948 that has left an enduring mark on the company:

"As our business grows, it becomes increasingly necessary to delegate responsibility and to encourage men and women to exercise their initiative. This requires considerable tolerance. Those men and women, to whom we delegate authority and responsibility, if they are good people, are going to want to do their jobs in their own way.

"Mistakes will be made, but if a person is essentially right, the mistakes he or she makes are not as serious, in the long run, as the mistakes management will make if it's dictatorial...

"Management that is destructively critical when mistakes are made kills initiative, and it is essential that we have many people with initiative if we are to continue to grow."

CONCLUSION

Innovation in the real world is never orderly. It is, after all, an intensely human process and at times managed with a degree of chaos. Sometimes management's actions can get in the way. The trick is to find the right balance and we've found that innovation works best if you:

- *Develop products for customers' future needs;*

- *Insist on a world-class development process; and, above all else;*

- *Realise the ability to succeed depends on people.*

If companies cannot adapt to change they will not survive. Innovation enables corporations not only to survive but also to succeed.

Chapter 3

Innovating for success

PART ONE: IDENTIFYING THE TALENT

The Millennium Products initiative, created by the Design Council in 1997, generated a groundswell of activity among the UK's most innovative companies, as documented in the Sharing Innovation research carried out this year. Andrew Summers, chief executive, Design Council, reports

One thousand British companies, one thousand breakthroughs: the Millennium Products initiative was launched in 1997 by Prime Minister Tony Blair to challenge UK businesses to submit products that exemplified contemporary British innovation and creativity.

The challenge attracted thousands of submissions, which were assessed by a panel of experts from business, science, engineering, media, culture and design. The panel members selected products and services they considered to be truly innovative, forward-thinking and problem solving. They chose only those products on the market after January 1995. Final submissions were received in November 1999 and, in all, 1,012 became Millennium Products.

But the initiative did not end as the new millennium arrived. It was seen early on that the stories behind these products could offer valuable insights into the innovation process and help organisations develop a culture where innovation could thrive.

The Design Council launched Sharing Innovation to explore and examine the stories behind Millennium Products. The results offer extraordinary insights into the way innovation happens. All UK companies can now tap into the secrets of innovation from

Britain's most creative companies, learning from the successes as well as the mistakes of innovation at the cutting edge

Sharing Innovation aims to foster a culture of innovation. Just one glance at the way so many leading companies run their business shows that success comes from having invested in and fostered an innovative culture. Sharing Innovation is about helping all companies to fast-track into that culture. It encompasses a whole programme of activities developed from the Design Council's Millennium Products initiative.

It also aims to encourage innovators to work together for mutual benefit and to help businesses and students learn how to create better, smarter products. Comprising the successful companies behind each Millennium Product, the Sharing Innovation Business Network is a community that will provide a forum for companies to share new ideas and new approaches.

Education resources are being developed to help students at all levels understand and practise innovation. At secondary school level, for example, students will be given physical examples of innovative products so that they can learn through hands-on experience.

The Design Council is also sharing British innovation with the world, creating in partnership with the Foreign and Commonwealth Office and British Council a series of international exhibitions that are telling the world about the innovation and creativity of UK business. Millennium Products exhibitions have toured Australia, Brunei, China, Europe, India, Korea, South Africa, South America and Singapore.

Following on from Sharing Innovation, the DTI's Future & Innovation Unit has worked closely with the Design Council to carry out an in-depth investigation into the practices behind the success of over 50 Millennium Product companies. A preview of the findings are detailed in Part Two.

PART TWO: VALUABLE LESSONS

Nigel Crouch, an industrialist with the DTI's Future & Innovation Unit, previews the powerful findings of Living Innovation, in-depth research into how Millennium Product companies have achieved outstanding results through innovation

Penicillin, the computer, microwave ovens and the World Wide Web are just four examples of UK world-beating creativity that instantly spring to mind. Unfortunately, however, while these were invented here they were developed elsewhere in the world...

LIVING INNOVATION

The UK's track record for successfully exploiting ideas and turning them into highly lucrative UK innovations is appalling. How, then, do we bridge the gap between inspired invention and fully-fledged innovation? Encouragingly, the answer lies very close to home with a number of British Millennium Product companies, who have contributed to the Living Innovation programme being run by the Future and Innovation Unit of the DTI in conjunction with the Design Council. This takes a look behind the innovation processes at work over a broad cross-section of Millennium Products and has generated some rich pointers as to how to innovate more effectively.

INNOVATION GOES STRAIGHT TO THE BOTTOM LINE

What has been particularly striking in Living Innovation is the dramatic impact effective innovation has on bottom-line performance. In many of the organisations we visited, innovation has literally transformed the business. Take Ragdoll Productions, the £22m company that has created highly successful children's television programmes including *Rosie and Jim*, *Tots TV* and the *Teletubbies*. It has always considered innovation as absolutely endemic to the business and has seen turnover and profits increase ten-fold over the last three years. Dolland and Aitchison, the high street opticians and spectacle retailer is another example. The company, which is totally committed to innovation, cite it as being both the key to the company's survival in 1996 and, against the backdrop of a static market, the platform for sales growth of 17 per cent and significantly increased market share over the past three years.

KEY QUESTIONS

Any business might find itself asking the following questions:

- Are you creating the right climate for innovation in your organisation and do you really know what your customer wants?

- Are you constrained by finance?

- Do you generate and capture good ideas and then take those ideas forward successfully through the organisation despite the many barriers that often exist?

- Do you make best use of teams and supplier and other networks?

- How well do you manage risk?

- Are you protecting your competitive advantage and, in particular, how well do you manage intellectual property rights?

- Is regulation a threat or an opportunity?

Living Innovation will help to answer all these questions, because it can provide hundreds of practical examples and hints from the outstanding companies visited on how to perform better in all these areas (and more).

THE MESSAGES FROM LIVING INNOVATION

The essence of successful innovation comes down to three key elements:

- *Unique understanding of customers and markets;*

- *An outstanding capability to implement;*

- *Inspirational and cultural leadership.*

However, it is essential that a company gets all of them right in order to make that critical difference to its bottom line.

UNIQUE UNDERSTANDING OF CUSTOMERS AND MARKETS

Company and customer united

The findings reveal that the traditional arm's length relationship has been replaced by a very close one. The following comments are very typical: "Customers were involved with the concept from the outset and kept informed of progress"; "We are very "customer intimate" – we spend a lot of our time and budget working with customers to ensure we are giving them something that really benefits them".

Another company used newspaper advertising to ask its customers: "What do you want from a firm in our business?" Others used service records, customer services and helplines to learn how they could better meet the needs of their customers. It was also common to find that user communities or electronic discussion groups had been set up to feed into the design decisions.

In Millennium Product companies, regulation is seen as an opportunity, not a threat. According to one respondent: "We are the only country that has these specifications and approval processes but it does mean the quality is better than anywhere else in the world. The British approval gives us a flag we can use around the world."

New market vision

A common strength of Millennium Product companies is their ability to spot new market opportunities beyond their usual confines and to pursue these with a vengeance.

One engineering company, that had already developed a new specialist UK application, had the vision to recognise that its product had more potential in a different, but wider, application. As a result, it totally redirected its marketing to exploit this.

Another challenged the established market model and, instead of just selling a product, started selling a service that sold the product. "This innovation changed the business and the entire profession beyond recognition. The competition is trying to catch up with similar initiatives but they are still a long way behind."

New market vision also means recognising when you need

to change the way you access your market. One respondent told us: "Our existing dealer network is no longer necessarily appropriate". Another commented: "We learned that our potential customers were not interested in buying from a firm in our industry. They wanted to use familiar suppliers, so we altered our strategy and selected a familiar supplier to help us in this area."

Knowing how to win

The companies we spoke to are extremely adept at keeping ahead of the competition. A number of factors come into play. They will willingly re-invent their business, if need be to best meet their customers' needs. "We set up a new company to differentiate between the new product range and our more traditional products".

There is also a major emphasis on adding value. "Our main focusing is on value-added processes. Anyone can make things but it is quality and design that are important".

And another key factor is managing intellectual property: "Getting control early of the IPR and the patent and licence situation has been paramount". But, there is no point having a patent if you can't police it. When a patent is not appropriate, an agreement with the relevant parties can be very effective.

AN OUTSTANDING CAPABILITY TO IMPLEMENT

Teaming with networks

As one would expect, successful organisations are heavily into cross-functional teams and high quality training for team leaders and team members. And while these companies work very hard at inter-team communication, they go beyond this by broadening the membership of teams to incorporate external partners, including customers and suppliers.

There is also considerable emphasis on physical co-location and the "passion factor" is also very important. "What really drove the innovation was the strong passion about the product."

At the same time, a company must have dogged determination and unshakeable commitment: "You need to approach innovation with the attitude that it's not going to beat you." It is also important that people have to really enjoy what they do and have a lot of fun.

"Hands ready" top management

A recurring issue among Millennium Product companies is the support of and commitment to innovation by top management. "The managing director was the driving force behind the development of the product," said one. At the same time, top management are giving people the necessary freedom to get on with the job. They will also reallocate resources – often quite dramatically – in order to help innovation to succeed.

Making it happen

Good ideas are clearly the lifeblood of successful innovation and the organisations participating in Living Innovation are very good at generating and capturing them. As well as using a variety of more formal approaches, these companies recognise that many ideas are spontaneous and come about informally.

The layout of the office can make a big difference to how well people spark off each other. The canteen and bar are also fertile breeding grounds for new ideas. It was also not uncommon to find one or two people in the organisation employed only to come up with big ideas: "You need crazy guys who think outside the box," confirmed one company.

Last but not least, too much specialist know-how can stifle essential lateral thinking: "We avoid people who know too much. They would have stopped us doing things," said another.

Another key finding from Living Innovation is that in order to be really successful, companies need to be willing to take a level of controlled risk. Sensible safeguards include having regular project review procedures in place and ensuring that innovation is closely linked to the company's vision and strategy. However, you still have to have the courage to stick your neck out at times. According to one respondent: "If the strategy is right, we will find a way to get the numbers right!"

Another firm put it this way: "We felt that we could and should do it but that it wouldn't be easy." And another said: "You have to have an element of breaking the rules or at least bending them...whether and when to bend the rules is still very much down to gut feel."

Finally, finance can sometimes be a problem, particularly for smaller companies operating at the high street level. However, for most of the companies participating in Living Innovation it was generally not seen to be an issue.

INSPIRATIONAL AND CULTURAL LEADERSHIP

What's it like to work here?

A culture for innovation is hard to achieve but it is critical to success. However, the following response represents the situation in many of the Millennium Product companies: "Our culture is professional, friendly, open, equal. It is also demanding, empowering, inspirational, motivational, challenging and supportive."

These organisations typically have very open communications, a culture built on total trust, an ethos that encourges everyone to challenge decisions and a fierce resistance to bureaucracy. "One facet of our organisation is that red tape doesn't get in the way." Furthermore, change is strongly embraced: "We promote an atmosphere where change is positively welcomed."

Stretching to achieve

The organisations also highlighted a willingness to step into the unknown as a key to success. Once again, the commitment to this has come from the top with senior level executives living up to the principle themselves: "The chairman had the vision to go with the project when prudent advice was that it was too risky."

Inspirational leadership imbues people with a burning zeal to create something really special. One company described their concept of a "restless company" where people ask, "What can we do to make it better?" as soon as a project is launched.

The research also highlighted the benefits of a truly blame-free management style: "There is a no-blame culture if an idea fails to live up to expectations." But, at the same time, management have a responsibility to ensure that risk is contained within sensible limits: "We believe it is a management failure if someone gets into a position where they make a terrible mistake."

Our people make us what we are

Successful innovating companies are extremely good at genuinely recognising their people's achievements and properly rewarding people financially: "The chief executive has a commitment to use talent and reward talent within the organisation," said one. However, the same respondent emphasised that non-financial recognition can be highly innovative. It runs a scheme where staff are encouraged to nominate others for an "incredible colleague" award.

WHERE NEXT?

The full findings from Living Innovation will reveal hundreds of practical examples of how some companies are consistently achieving brilliant innovation. In the meantime, guidance can be obtained at www.innovation. gov.uk/pwp and at www.sharing innovation.org.uk.

The last word on this crucial issue of innovation goes to the company who put it this way: "Don't do it unless you have a passion for it!"

1 To improve on sand...

EXAMPLE OF CONVENTIONAL SANDPAPER AT 120X

2 We created the pyramids.

EXAMPLE OF TRIZACT ABRASIVES AT 250X

And they aren't the kind you'd find in Egypt! Millions of identical microscopic pyramids make up 3M™ Trizact™Abrasives – a new class of efficient abrasives that are a leap beyond sandpaper. Using our patented process of microreplication, Trizact abrasives can shape parts of a jet engine to 1/10,000 of an inch. We find new ways to smooth out the rough spots by making the leap *from need to...*

3M™ Trizact™
Abrasives

3M *Innovation*

Chapter 4

New ways of working

In an increasingly competitive global market companies need to break down barriers and forge new types of partnership with academic institutions, suppliers and even competitors. Henrietta Lake, business writer, reports

Rules are made to be broken. Nowhere is this truer than in current business practice. Companies are being forced to learn new ways of working together, using approaches that even a few years ago would have been unthinkable.

Competitor no longer means adversary and an employee does not just clock out at the end of the day. Former bastions of "impartial" advice, such as lawyers, accountants and strategic consultants, are taking equity stakes in their client companies and creating a whole new dynamic to this relationship. Bigger no longer means better as large blue-chip firms are forming equal partnerships with start-ups. Many companies are striking ever-closer links with other organisations, while some are even collaborating with their competitors. This rush to alliances is a common strategic response to globalisation, competition and technological change.

According to Alan Barrell a venture capitalist at NW Brown, the Cambridge-based financial services firm, the convergence of technologies is creating companies without a definable centre and resulting in networks replacing hierarchical organisations.

These networks may be real or virtual, between business and academia or between customers and suppliers, but the result is the same: a whole new way of doing business.

Traditional business sense dictates that a competitor is just that. On no account should dialogue, let alone a joint venture, be entered into. After all, you could lose some of your advantage.

It is certainly counter-intuitive to join forces with your rivals, but think about the alternative. Innovative businesses are busily building partnerships because they recognise it is the only route to survival. Many of the supermarket and major retail chains, for example, are collaborating on a project called efficient consumer response (ECR). While theirs remains a highly competitive industry, companies such as Sainsburys, Asda, and Tesco have teamed up for joint gains by further streamlining their supply chains.

The initiative is built around the principle of creating common industry standards. This is being done in areas such as data collection, which will enable valuable information to be easily studied and used across the whole industry. It is also being implemented in the design of standardised (and re-useable) crates and pallets, the consolidation of products in jointly owned ware-houses and even in the sharing of distribution lorries.

Innovation and evolving technologies are also encouraging new types of company – ones with no definable boundaries – to come into existence.

VIRTUOUS CIRCLE

Red Fig, a London-based technology firm, has developed an interactive giant screen that sits on the front of a building or an advertising board

The screen not only presents video and text information via computer, but also becomes interactive for anyone who uses a mobile phone to dial an advertised number.

Red Fig is a technology consultant in essence, albeit one which has designed an innovative and highly versatile new product. But because each of its projects uses a host of media applications – mobile telecommunications, television broadcast technology, network operators and content providers – the company relies on strategic alliances with a minimum of four other companies each time. And while Red Fig continues to hold the intellectual property to the technology, it is difficult to tell on any one project where one company's work and responsibility ends and another's begins.

This inclusive approach is also being utilised within more traditional business relationships such as those between customers and suppliers. Having cut out the waste within their own organisations many, typically large, firms are looking for other ways to reduce costs, which most often can only be done by collaborating with suppliers. By synchronising manufacture and production processes along supply chains, production and distribution costs can be substantially reduced. This can be done by co-ordinating the turnaround times of lorries, by using automatic ordering systems or even the more sophisticated intranets which enable suppliers to anticipate repeat orders by monitoring their customer's warehouse stock or in-store supplies.

Two companies that have done pioneering work in this area are Nissan and Unipart. Both have realised that their success depends on their relationship with suppliers as well as customers. They have developed ways of assessing and improving the relationship with suppliers, encouraging other companies to implement these new purchaser/supplier models within their own organisations.

TEN-POINT PLAN

Unipart has invested time and effort with employees and suppliers to demonstrate that working together brings costs down through the supply chain

The company's initial investigations into the working of its supply chain exposed, for example, the dangers of a once-a-year price-negotiation relationship with suppliers: to stay cheap, suppliers cut corners and reduced quality, which led to business failure on both sides.

To combat this problem it introduced a stakeholder approach and the Ten-to-Zero (TTZ) relationship programme. Ten key elements between the customer and supplier are appraised so that progress on each can be monitored over time. Teams are then put together from both companies to work on improvements along the supply chain for mutual benefit.

Unipart argues that the TTZ programme takes the politics out of supplier assessment and motivates suppliers to learn from each other. The company also claims that every one-point advancement on the TTZ measurement scale saves it £500,000.

Improved communication techniques are taking place not only between old partners such as purchasers and suppliers, but also between worlds as far apart as industry and academia.

Links between higher education and industry have been growing steadily over the last ten years, from university-based science parks and incubation centres to collaborative research projects, all with encouragement from government. However, there is some way to go before Britain manages to recreate the success stories witnessed in the US at Stanford University or the Massachusetts Institute of Technology. Each is estimated to have spawned a trillion dollars worth of companies, centred around Silicon Valley and Cambridge in Boston, respectively.

A MEETING OF MINDS

The St John's Innovation Centre in Cambridge has so far produced one of the best, although by no means the only, UK model for collaborative efforts between business and academia. A study by Segal Quince Wicksteed, the consultancy firm, found that more than a third of local, small companies in Cambridge said that university connections and research were significant to their work and growth.

As in all good partnerships, these new collaborative efforts are a two-way process. Companies that cannot afford to fund, or do not have the expertise in-house to develop their own research and development facilities, can obtain this from the universities. Meanwhile, the universities have a new method of generating income and the ability to commercialise some of their own research through new partnerships with industry.

Perhaps one of the most blatant examples of a new approach to business practice is the emergence of a multitude of so-called business incubators modelled on the early examples started by the universities.

Incubators are designed as hothouses for new, ambitious companies and typically provide business and technical advice and contacts in order to kick-start a firm's growth. The young companies may be physically situated close together in one building

PROGRESSIVE PARTNERSHIPS

British Aerospace Systems and Equipment (BASE) was only able to develop its silicon gyroscope through close collaboration with academia

The gyroscope is an instrument that can sense minute movements in all directions and has applications in everything from advanced car brake systems and safety airbags, to 3D computer mice. When used in a braking system the gyroscope can sense if the car is about to go into a skid or roll and immediately applies the brakes.

But in order to create a gyroscope which would be inexpensive enough for wide use by commercial car manufacturers and rugged enough to withstand large shocks – for use by the military – the technicians at BASE had to approach academics for assistance. Nottingham University supplied the know-how on gyro theory and Cranfield and Loughborough universities the manufacturing advice. BASE also formed partnerships with the Sowerby Research Centre in Bristol for the fundamental research on silicon.

or the incubator may be "virtual" and merely a web of expertise and contacts that the member companies can draw on.

Examples of one new form of incubator, being built outside an academic environment, have been set up by the management consultancy firms. These include Bain Lab and Accelerator, run by Bain and McKinsey respectively. The consultancies are using their business expertise, and contacts with accountants, venture capitalists and other professionals, in order to jump-start fast-growth firms, while hoping to reap substantial rewards by sharing in the incubated firm's future success.

BORN TO BE WIRED

Incubators are also being developed between the entrepreneurs themselves. Ideas Hub was set up for internet entrepreneurs by internet entrepreneurs, to help rapidly develop new business ideas into successful companies. This Cambridge-based incubator provides seed investment together with the services, development resources and industry networks, critical to the successful nurturing of an internet start-up.

Other forms of incubator can be based on products that the young company actually needs, such as the aptly named business-incubator.com – a collaboration between Cisco, Oracle, Sun Microsystems, and Exodus Communications. This incubator allows internet start-ups to minimise the technical barriers of becoming an e-business by offering a cheap, secure, reduced-risk environment, to develop and test e-trading systems for three months before launching a company.

STEADY GROWTH

Nextweekend.com, an internet start-up that enables users to plan their leisure time, is one of business-incubator.com's first "babies"

The incubator has allowed the company to test its ideas and infrastructure before going live. Chris Moss, the firm's chief executive, explains: "One of the temptations with the internet is to roll everything out at once. However, as with any business venture, success depends on planning and execution. By working closely with the business-incubator.com partners and pooling our collective experiences we anticipate an imminent, successful launch in the UK."

Collaboration brings strength in many aspects of business, particularly when developing new companies. Many of the new internet start-ups cannot afford to waste valuable time by gaining experience through "old-fashioned" trial and error. Instead, they need to rely on alliances with other companies that are experienced in their fields. Because the potential gains are so tremendous over the long term, the larger firms are prepared to provide their services often at a greatly reduced cost.

It is undoubtedly the innovative and successful companies of the future which have realised that in today's business environment it is harmful, not to say foolish, to ignore the possibilities of partnership or collaboration. Something might have to give in return – a piece of the equity, a share in the profits, or the divulging of proprietary information. But, in the end, many would contend that without these alliances they would simply be failing to exploit their potential to grow and thrive.

People, culture and teamworking

Sustained innovation can only be achieved if there is an open company culture that nurtures ideas and contributions from all individuals. But, says Tim Melville-Ross, chairman of Investors in People, teamworking is also essential

Innovation and creativity have long been a principal way for businesses to improve their competitive edge. But how can they generate an environment and method of working which fosters and encourages such a climate?

Let's start with a few observations. First, we need to establish whose responsibility it is to innovate. Businesses that confine this activity to the R&D department are surely missing out. By drawing on the input, experience and ideas of everyone involved in the business, organisations benefit from the application of a wider pool of knowledge.

By the same token, small companies that lack an official R&D team can maximise often limited resources by encouraging all employees to contribute ideas. It is also worth noting that innovations need not simply apply to the creation of new products and services. A creative approach to devising more effective and efficient business processes can be just as valuable.

If we accept that organisations that encourage creative input from everyone are likely to perform better, the next issue is how to motivate people to make innovative contributions. And, finally, given the existence of an inclusive, open culture, what methods and practices should be employed to manage this process successfully.

Much has been written on the subject of motivation. It is now recognised widely that no single factor alone will deliver motivated staff. Surveys have continually demonstrated that job satisfaction can rank higher than remuneration as a motivator.

At a simple – but extremely important – level, it is possible to argue that all personnel need clear answers to the following questions if an employer is to reap the rewards of a motivated and creative workforce:

■   *What do you want me to do?*

■   *Why do I have to do it?*

■   *How should I do it?*

■   *How am I getting on?*

■   *What is in it for me?*

The way a business communicates the answers to these questions must fit with its working needs. Team briefings, one-on-one sessions with line managers, staff away-days, etc. are all useful tools. But a workforce that is made up of individuals who understand how their contribution and activities are aligned to, and impact on, the achievement of organisational goals is far more likely to develop a business focus.

This approach of employee involvement has already been widely adopted by more than 37,000 UK organisations currently working with Investors in People. This is the national Standard that sets a level of good practice for aligning business strategy with people strategy for the benefit of both.

CREATING THE RIGHT CLIMATE

By recognising staff's contribution, supporting their development needs and making them aware of the business's needs, a company can help to create a climate that actively encourages innovation across the board. Motivated people are the ones who get to see how their individual successes translate into overall business success and feel rewarded for it. They are also the employees who will seize the initiative and suggest changes and innovations to processes or tasks where they see that improvements can be made.

An open culture, where everyone is encouraged to contribute regardless of his or her "status", also requires a commitment from senior management that people are not being asked to come up with solutions and innovations simply as a means to introduce staff cuts. While redundancies are, sadly, a fact of business life, the motivation to contribute will not last long if the direct result is a hatchet job on employee numbers.

Ultimately, an open culture will not exist without good communication, horizontally and vertically. It is not enough just to ensure good information flow between line managers and their direct reports. Inter-departmental communication is crucial if a holistic approach to strategy development and implementation is to succeed. At a task level, it is also vital that individuals appreciate the demands not just of their own jobs but of others too. This kind of understanding, which can be achieved through a variety of means such as job shadowing, can encourage people to suggest innovations beyond their immediate job remit.

A SHARED COMMITMENT

So, how should organisations encourage an open culture with the purpose of stimulating innovation and initiative? The answer lies in effective team building and teamworking. Individuals should always feel encouraged to submit a "bright idea", but creating teams to address specific innovation needs can also be a highly productive way of making operational improvements and enabling staff to acquire new skills.

The existence of teams can help to build an open culture by bringing everybody together, at junior and senior level. It helps to generate a sense of common purpose, responsibility and a shared commitment to the achievement of goals. It means that employees from different areas of the business get the chance to collaborate – giving them an improved understanding of their colleagues' needs. As a result, staff tend to be more supportive of each other at work and are better equipped to help each other in the event of problems.

The benefits to the innovation process are numerous. Teams provide good conditions in which to discuss and analyse problems, brainstorm new ideas and encourage the input of creative thought.

All round, a team approach by its nature creates a cross-fertilisation of thinking and this is its principal benefit. Members may adopt different roles from those of their "normal job", drawing on and enhancing skills that they have formed outside the workplace.

But before pursuing the concept of team working, it is worth stressing the difference between a team and a group of people. A group is made up of a collection of people who have come together for a mixture of social, practical or professional reasons (friends, family, etc). Their association is not pre-planned in a way that accounts for the mix of skills and abilities within.

A team, on the other hand, is formed in order to accomplish a common purpose, and must be put together with care. By focusing on the importance of team selection, building and team leadership, organisations can help to engender an open culture and at the same time assist, manage and evaluate innovation and problem solving.

R. Meredith Belbin, one of the leading researchers into team dynamics, has identified that in order for teams to be effective they need to be made up of a balance of personality types and competencies. He categorises eight roles which are found to exist within effective teams:

- *Chair: a social leader and co-ordinator;*

- *Shaper: an extrovert, dominant task leader;*

- *Company worker: a practical, efficient organiser who gets on with things;*

- *Resource investigator: a good negotiator and diplomat;*

- *Plant: creative thinker and ideas person;*

- *Monitor-evaluator: an analyst who monitors results and outcomes;*

- *Team worker: non-competitive, mediator;*

- *Completer-finisher: progress chaser, checker of details and deadlines.*

While in the real world it may not always be possible to form teams that reflect precisely this breakdown, organisations can certainly increase the likelihood of team success by considering and acting on the following:

■ *Pinpoint where potential team members may be lacking in skills or experience and identify how this can be addressed. (Get the team itself to make suggestions).*

■ *Ensure the competencies of the team members are aligned with their responsibilities and creative brief.*

■ *Identify how the team's actions will affect others in the organisation and inform them.*

■ *Make sure fellow employees are made aware of the team's achievements.*

THE BEAUTY OF BRAINSTORMING

The innovation process is often kickstarted by a personal interest or hobby, and can involve the adaptation of the unlikeliest technologies to a completely different market

So it was with Valpar Industrial Limited, whose directors' interest in the marine industry inspired them to take materials previously used for drinks dispensers and turn them into a fendering system attached to pontoons to protect boat hulls.

To research the viability of their product the directors used key people at customer level to get feedback on the kinds of problems that they were having with current technology and carried out basic product trials to get a feel for how the market would react. This helped them to focus the product in that direction.

"We constantly networked and tested our ideas and concepts with everyone who would listen, and used this as a method of fine-tuning the final product," explains Valpar's Commercial Director Karen Beckett. "We also got multi-functional groups together to brainstorm and look at all the options."

To encourage further innovation the company holds regular product and process development meetings and tries to get everyone involved.

It is sensible to consider how the progress of a good team and its "innovative output" should be measured and evaluated. If the team has been built properly, its members will have defined and become committed to key milestones and overall goals. This makes progress easy to monitor. Feedback becomes more meaningful as team members know what is expected of them and can track their own outputs. As a result, a teamworking culture enables organisations to plan and evaluate the achievement of collective task-based problem solving or innovation and personal progress.

It is this mix of collective and personal development that makes a team-based approach to problem solving such a good environment for fostering a culture of continuous improvement. Individuals develop to meet team needs and the team achieves more through the sum of the developing skills of its members. Ultimately, this can be summed up as improving organisational performance through people development – a strategy that is the way to modern business success.

Knowledge management

The primary role of knowledge management for a company should be to support product innovation. But says John Howells, technical director of 3M, United Kingdom, this is a cultural and organisational issue rather than a technological one

As the debate on knowledge management has increased in recent years, so has the level of confusion over what it means for business. Surely we've been gathering knowledge for centuries – and applying what we know to improve and learn something new from the experience?

This is true, but the difference for today's practitioner is the pace of change. New technologies facilitate the capture, manipulation and exchange of information. Product lifecycles are shortening and global competition is increasing. The reward to a company is not power itself but the key to gaining real competitive advantage. No wonder, then, that knowledge management is a rapidly developing area of best business practice.

DEFINING KNOWLEDGE

Companies and their employees generate two types of knowledge. Traditional work processes are designed to capture and disseminate explicit knowledge. This is well structured, formal and highly organised. Tacit knowledge, however, is less straightforward. Based on intuition, it is only gained by personal observation and firsthand experience. It is precisely this knowledge, however difficult to capture and organise, that gives companies the edge.

But both types of knowledge share one crucial dynamic: the need to interpret rather than merely collect information. Knowledge remains nothing without understanding.

Knowledge management determines how effectively a company uses its intellectual assets. In simple terms it involves generating knowledge, from inside and outside the organisation, and then exploiting it to gain competitive advantage.

Successful knowledge management can enable companies to build customer loyalty, brand reputation and create patents. It equips companies with the ability to maximise the return on investment, respond to market demands, plan for the future, or even just survive. Take the example of Ford Motor Company, whose Best Practice Replication web site contains more than 2,600 proven practices. The company has identified over $950m projected value over the next three years.

Today's regulatory bodies attach so much importance to intangible assets such as knowledge that a recent Financial Reporting Standard stated that British companies must report their intangible assets if they are measurable. For this reason alone, it is vital that companies look to understand and measure the value of intellectual capital.

CREATING THE RIGHT CULTURE

But all too often knowledge management is talked about in abstract, esoteric terms. Over-wrought business theories already abound and "KM" threatens to spawn new acronyms. And the power of technology tempts us into believing that knowledge can be controlled through systems. In reality, however, sharing knowledge and exchanging information and experience is a highly personal process. It is people, not technology, who translate knowledge into understanding.

Companies need to create a culture in which knowledge management can thrive. Building an environment where individuals not only can but are willing to share information with each other, is something that a company can control. Horizontal sharing of knowledge cuts right across the instincts and culture of many businesses, yet in the quest for "breakthrough" discoveries, it is the only way that organisations can hope, collectively, to match the achievements of individual genius. However, the belief that knowledge is power can easily make employees reluctant to share ideas, particularly if a company places too great an emphasis on rewarding individual performance. An effective culture, therefore, will reward both individual effort and promote knowledge sharing.

It is also important to stress that employees who leave an organisation take their knowledge with them, so every effort needs to be made to maximise key staff retention. Moreover, an atmosphere of generosity, freedom and safety needs to be nurtured since innovation works best when employees trust their company to repay loyalty over time. Such in-depth knowledge and experience cannot be duplicated quickly by competitors, even if they have sophisticated knowledge management systems in place.

An infrastructure built on technology makes it possible to leverage the creative "grey cells" of people and provide a supportive environment that engages human interaction and collaboration. Ovum analysts forecast that the worldwide market for knowledge management software is set to increase from the 1999 level of $515m to $3.5bn by 2004. More and more employees will move away from information to knowledge work.

But having all the databases in the world guarantees nothing in itself. While computers can transfer knowledge around the world in seconds, one of the biggest challenges faced by an organisation is managing the sheer volume of information. The aim should be to "get 80 per cent of the benefit for 20 per cent of the effort," suggested Ian Black, head of communications, BAE SYSTEMS when the company launched its corporate university. Technology is there to help, but users must exploit what it can offer and understand what they need to know in order to add business value.

MADE FOR SHARING

Sources of new knowledge are often external, such as suppliers or customers, which raises the question of knowledge protection. Should a company convert some of its confidential information, or intellectual capital, or look to guard this valuable knowledge? It's a trade-off. One approach that 3M supports is Innovation Partnering, an active network of companies, suppliers, research

BUILDING A KNOWLEDGE COMMUNITY

3M recognises that employees are more likely to respond to a request for knowledge or support if they know one another. So it has developed multiple processes to facilitate the sharing of tacit knowledge.

The company employs a host of communications media, including IT systems, e-mail and video conferencing, and has never forgotten the good old-fashioned technique of one-on-one dialogue. By sharing knowledge and insights within and outside the organisation, many of our best-loved and most successful products have been developed.

Certain 3M "heroes of innovation" are well known within the company and the tradition of "story-telling" serves to sustain the culture of knowledge sharing so that the company learns from both successful and unsuccessful projects and applies that knowledge in later work.

It has also created communities of excellence, called Technology Centres. The worldwide 3M technical community gathers regularly, to present and share work and ideas with one another, and Technical Audits are structured to help networking and transfer knowledge from one 3M business to another.

Senior management is responsible for ensuring that the organisational culture encourages knowledge sharing and for signposting the types of knowledge that matter most. Knowledge management priorities are also linked to business targets – for example, to generate 30 per cent of sales from products introduced in the last four years.

specialists and customers who collaborate together to accelerate the transfer of knowledge and the development of technical applications.

Government too has a crucial role to play if British businesses are to compete with the best in the world. A knowledge management unit within the Department of Trade and Industry is planned, to capture best practice and identify the knowledge management needs of small businesses.

The internet has made it technologically possible to capture knowledge and make it widely available, cost effectively. Yet2.com is one web-based "go-between" among sellers and would-be buyers of technologies and intellectual property. And with technology licensing available on the internet, companies can benefit in simple revenue terms from allowing access to their technologies. But the real value may be in forming new liaisons around such global meeting places, to fully exploit a technology platform into new products and services.

CONCLUSION

It has never been more important for companies to exploit their own sources of knowledge to serve new customers and markets. The speed with which companies apply what they know will drive their future competitiveness. Knowledge is at the heart of innovation and, in the words of Tom Peters, "the only sustainable competitive advantage is to out-innovate the competition".

Technology, systems and processes must play their part, but knowledge management, in the final analysis, rests on brainpower, understanding and the application of that information. In this context, people, organisation and culture will continue to hold the key.

Sponsor a Director's Guide

With more than 50 titles produced, the Director's Guide series is a highly successful business publishing venture

Each guide is produced in conjunction with a major blue-chip sponsor – from Oracle and Grant Thornton to Cable & Wireless and Fedex – and each is sent free to 50,000 individual members of the IoD in the UK.

Director's Guides cover a diverse range of topics – from e-commerce to growth finance, from customer care to management buy-outs. Research shows the series forms a key part of IoD members' business reading, with a high retention value and pass-on readership. The direct benefits to the sponsor include:

- *50,000 individual director-level circulation*
- *Strong position as an authority in its specialist area*
- *Authorship of three chapters*
- *Full co-branding with the IoD*
- *Seven pages of exclusive advertising, including two colour positions on the covers*
- *A reply-paid card bound into the guide, for direct response*
- *3,000 sponsor copies*
- *Broad press coverage*

For further enquiries, please contact
Business Development and Sponsorship on:
020 7766 8555
or e-mail us at busdev@iod.co.uk

Chapter 7

The customer and the supply chain

Customer and supplier input in innovation is vital, says Peter Bartram, business and technology writer. A company can use this information to refine designs, solve problems and develop product lines

When it comes to fishermen's tales, the best are always about the one that got away. But Andrew England-Kerr, director of Englands, designers and suppliers of specialist safety equipment, has a tale with a difference. His is about an idea for a self-inflating fishing jacket – the Doctor's Jacket – that saves lives. Luckily it didn't get away and Kerr has brought his company further success on the back of this innovative product.

As England-Kerr has found, there is nothing like feedback from customers to help a company develop its existing products and think of new ones. He is delighted that people still write to tell him that they've survived an accident because they were wearing a Doctor's Jacket.

OUT WITH THE OLD, IN WITH THE NEW

But the way in which companies keep in touch with customers is changing fast in the face of new business and technology forces. And as more varied ways of reaching customers emerge, the traditional supply chain is under threat. To thrive in the future, companies will have to follow new rules, focusing on being as innovative in managing the different components of their supply chains as they are in developing mind-blowing new products.

There are two key issues which are changing the shape of supply chains and the way they work. Each alters the type and quality of interaction a company might have with different members of its supply chain and with end-customers.

The first key issue is the way in which marketplaces are evolving into "market-spaces". The wider use of IT and the emergence of e-business means that it's not now so important where some businesses operate from. Many will succeed as well, if not better, with a web site rather than a store in the high street.

SPACE IS WHERE IT'S AT

The theory of market-spaces was first expounded in the 1990s in the *Harvard Business Review* by two US academics, J F Rayport and J J Sviokla. They argued that in a market-space the content of a transaction can be different because, instead of purchasing the product, you buy some information. So, rather than buying the *Financial Times*, you look at it online. Similarly, "consumers" download music from a web site rather than buying a CD.

In many instances person-to-person interactions are being replaced by a screen. This is potentially bad news for those businesses, such as Englands, which rely heavily on personal customer feedback. Unless, of course, they can find a way to get that feedback as they sell their products over the web. But those businesses that develop highly sophisticated web-based selling can collect immensely detailed information about the preferences of their customers and what sells as a by product of the sale. Those companies that become really clever at learning about what their customers want will be able to wow them with detailed knowledge about their preferences.

Lynette Ryals, a teaching fellow in marketing at Cranfield School of Management, tells the story of a First Direct bank customer who telephoned a query about cashpoint facilities in a ski resort. When he returned from holiday, he rang the bank again about something else, spoke to a different operator and was asked: "Did you have a good skiing holiday?" Some customers might find that rather spooky, but it illustrates the power that a company has to communicate with customers in "market-space".

There are other ways in which changes in the supply chain are not quite so clear to read. In theory, it's great news that technology is making it so much easier to communicate directly with customers.

Get to know 3M

Please tick as many boxes as you wish

☐ Yes, please send me more information about 3M

☐ Yes, I would like to know more about 3M technologies/technology partnering

☐ Yes, I would like to know more about innovation at 3M

☐ Yes, please send me some information on 3M Solutions for:-

Architecture & Construction

Home & Leisure

Office

Creative Communications

Education

Utilities & Telecom

Manufacturing & Industrial

Safety

Electronics Manufacture

Automotive, Marine & Aerospace

Health Care

Other

Web Site: www.3M.com/uk ● Phone 08705 360036
e-mail: innovation@uk.mmm.com

Title

Forename

Surname

Job title

Company

Nature of business

Address

Post Code

Tel:

Fax:

e-mail

3M *Innovation*

Corporate Communications
3M United Kingdom PLC
3M House, PO Box 1
Market Place
Bracknell
Berkshire
RG12 1ZU

But that might not be such good news if your company sits somewhere in the middle of the primary manufacturer and the end-customer.

There is certainly a temptation to cut out the middle men and seek to forge direct relationships with the final customers. For some companies, that will clearly be an important option. And dot.com businesses are predicated on the ability to telescope the supply chain together. But even these enterprises have to find a way of getting goods from the warehouse to the customer.

Adabra.com, a web-based community shopping site, overcame the problem by forging a partnership with distribution giant Securicor. And, innovatively, it ensures that goods are delivered in the evenings when customers are more likely to be at home.

CHANGING WITH THE TIDES

There are also opportunities to redesign "upstream" supply chains – towards suppliers rather than customers – in order to deliver better value for money. Jaguar Cars, for example, now works more closely with suppliers to share design information when it's developing new models. It started with its headlamp suppliers and constructed a knowledge-based computer model that contains information about the design, manufacturing and costing process. Using this model, Jaguar engineers configure the headlamp supplier's lighting during the concept styling of new models. They are able to resolve many of the fitting and functional issues more quickly – and without the need for so many consultations with the supplier.

Such examples illustrate the enormous potential for changing the balance of power in supply chains. The companies that have more power will need to use it wisely, while those in a weaker position will need to discover ways to deliver more value to their customers. Merlin Stone, a consultant specialising in customer relationship issues, believes that the key for many companies is to look at ways in which they can work with other members of their supply chain to deliver jointly more value to their end-customers. After all, every member of the supply chain should benefit if more end-customers buy the product or service as a result of the supply chain partners working together – whether that's Jaguar working with sub-assembly suppliers or a dot.com company with a distribution specialist.

At the heart of this debate, Stone argues, each company needs to understand how it can add value in the supply chain.

LOOKING FOR SUPPLY CHAIN LEVERAGE

Companies, especially intermediaries, in a supply chain can look at these ways to add value to the end-customer:

1. Showing the range. Providing an easy way for customers to view the products at a nearby location;

2. Delivering the product. Providing the logistics support to stock and/or deliver the product to the end-customer;

3. Managing the stock. Understanding customers' purchasing patterns so they can increase or decrease stock to meet peaks or troughs of demand;

4. Supporting the brand. Adding its own brand strength to those of the products it sells – as when a big store stocks a product from a little-known manufacturer;

5. Motivating to buy. Targeting individual customers whose previous purchasing pattern suggests they may be a target for a specific product;

6. Arranging a contract, when there's a need for a formal process to transfer title to the goods from the manufacturer to the customer;

7. Repackaging the product, when the supplier can only deliver in large amounts and there may be a need to break bulk in smaller quantities;

8. Handling customer risk, in deciding whether to sell or not to sell a product to a customer who might not pay for it or make unreasonable warranty claims;

9. Offering finance. Helping the customer to buy with a loan or easy-terms payments;

10. Dealing with complaints. Providing the first port of call for customers with a problem.

Recognising how to add value in the supply chain is particularly crucial for intermediaries downstream from the main manufacturer. Retailers should consider themselves a valuable source of information, not just about the products they sell, but also about new products that customers would like to buy.

In this way, retailers add more value by building themselves into the product development loop – and create opportunities for enhancing their own margins. For example, sports clothing retailers played a key role in providing customer feedback information for Acordis when it was developing Amicor+, an engineered fibre which inhibits bacteria and fungal growth. For Acordis, talking to retailers about what their customers were telling them was an important part of finding out what makes sports people feel comfortable and fresh – and, thus, what kind of garments they would like to wear.

Another key question is how to build a productive working relationship between product supplier and the intermediaries that help to get it into the customer's hands. One of the thorniest problems is often the "ownership" of the customer. As Merlin Stone highlights, even if the supplier's relationship with the customer is based purely on branding and product and the intermediary's is based on sales and service, each will be nervous about losing or diluting its relationship with final customers. His solution is that the parties develop a joint understanding of customer requirements, possibly using a trusted third-party – such as a database holder – as a link. They can then build programmes which encourage the customer to come to the intermediary for the supplier's product. It's also easier to share information, such as customer preferences, that is key in developing products and services in the future.

Increasingly, technology – such as the internet – makes it possible for partners to make joint propositions to customers. For example, some companies that use UPS to deliver their products place a UPS icon on their own web sites so that customers can track delivery progress. In this situation, the intermediary – UPS – is providing customer information the supplier would find impossible to offer itself.

Small and medium-sized companies, in particular, need to learn the near-political new skills of working with supply chain partners. Even if you're not selling life-saving fishing jackets, you still need to become a more skilled angler if you're to hook future customers.

GLOWING EXAMPLE OF COLLABORATION

It has always been the case that those companies that involve their customers in activities such as product design and implementation succeed best

In 1998 TDI Advertising launched its Electric Paper product – a kind of poster for the side of buses that illuminates when an electric current is passed through it. The idea came about after TDI consulted suppliers on new ways to improve advertising.

Electric Paper looked much better than the old pasted posters but the bus companies were worried that the current might interfere with the bus's own electrics. So TDI included representatives from the bus companies in its production team. Up close, they could see Electric Paper posed no technical threats and, therefore, bought into the project and the product.

Chapter 8

Innovation in e-services

In the Digital Age, companies of all sizes can rapidly gain market share through newer and better e-services. Marc Beishon, business and technology writer, offers some insights

It is a sign of the times to see fresh-faced e-business entrepreneurs popping up on *Question Time* or gracing the profile slots in the newspaper business pages. The reason is simple and common to all – innovation.

Everyone wants to know the "secret" of their success in the internet world, in the hope that it will rub off on them. In the same way that traditional businesses watched in amazement as the direct sellers set up telephone operations in the 1980s, so the new internet businesses are creating a similar seismic shock. Everyone knows about Amazon.com, the online book seller. Now add travel operation lastminute.com, internet bank Egg, CD music seller Boxman...the list grows longer each day.

Some of these businesses, notably Amazon, are yet to return a profit. But this is not unusual for start-up businesses, and there will undoubtedly be casualties, mergers and acquisitions aplenty as the e-business "dot.com" market takes shape. What these companies are bringing about are new ways of doing business – and if one company fails to make the most of an innovation, another surely will.

Take lastminute.com, the company that sells last-minute tickets for events, flights, hotel away breaks and even restaurant sittings. Founded in 1998, the company has a disarmingly simple aim: "To encourage spontaneous, romantic and occasionally adventurous behaviour. Live out your dreams at unbeatable prices."

The operative word, of course, is "spontaneous" – it is only by using a web site that the company can offer such a complete and dynamic list of last-minute things to do. No other medium comes close to the accessibility and presentational aspects that a web site affords from the customer's point of view. Furthermore, the internet allows the stock availability – the services on offer – to be updated from participating suppliers in real time.

It's a similar story at Amazon.com where books are not only offered at discount prices, but readers also post their own reviews – a brilliant coup to counter the self-serving blurb normally seen on the back jacket in a conventional bookshop.

It is this kind of touch that marks out the innovative e-business. And while each feature may not seem like much on its own, the overall make-up of a web site may cater for a breadth of users that is beyond the scope of a conventional store. It could be access – a rural dweller who can't get into town; it could be time – a precious commodity for most people; or it may be security and confidentiality, with people free to browse items they'd be embarrassed to be seen doing in public. For any of these people, the innovation could simply be in opening up a new avenue to get served.

Looking back on some of the UK's e-commerce pioneers, there is a small army of craft industries ranging from high-class cakes and confectionery to model soldiers and teddy bears. For these firms, a web site and e-mail has brought a powerful and growing new channel to their businesses, often with a worldwide dimension.

AUTOMATING THE SUPPLY CHAIN

Much of the talk about e-business innovation, of course, lies in the supplier-consumer relationship. Mention e-commerce and people usually think about the supply of goods and services to the public, and especially the increased reach the internet has brought to the smaller business.

The sophistication of e-commerce solutions is continually increasing, with sites such as lastminute.com demonstrating more elements of the true e-business solution, where the aim is to have all elements of the supply chain integrated into a seamless process. Orders are made online; stock availability checked; credit cards authorised; ledgers updated; stock re-ordered; warehouse and shipping instructions issued.

Automating the complete supply chain cycle is clearly a tremendous e-business innovation in its own right – and the business-to-business part of the cycle is reckoned by most analysts to be receiving more attention, and gaining more benefits, than the business-to-consumer part of the market.

Procurement, for example, is proving to be a logical first step for many companies in using new e-business techniques. Although companies have been using electronic transaction methods for purchasing for some time, "web-enabled" systems that use the internet add new, powerful dimensions to the process.

Companies can make sure employees view only items from approved catalogues on user-friendly browser interfaces. The catalogues can be updated often and linked to purchase order systems, automating the transactions with the supplier. What is more, new deals can be struck with suppliers to gain better discounts by committing to "approved status", so employees are given less opportunity to make rogue purchases that bust budgets.

SELF SERVICE

Deploying a web-style browser interface around a firm can provide a set of other e-business style benefits. Many companies are introducing "employee self-service" applications. These allow staff instant access to expense claim systems, travel booking, sickness and welfare systems, etc. There is no reason why internal systems can't be seen as e-business innovations in their own right.

Then there is the deployment of knowledge-based systems, which aim to capture the expertise that is often scattered around the company and allow the information to be used where it is needed most. Salespeople, for example, can access presentations for a particular type of meeting, whether this be material pre-loaded on a laptop computer or, increasingly, information accessed via a live internet wireless link.

So new methods can come in many different forms, a fact borne out by the categories in the annual BT e-business Innovation Awards, one of the most high-profile schemes in the UK. The award categories in 1999 included knowledge management and supply chain management but also customer service, collaborative working and interactive marketing.

GETTING TO KNOW YOU

Marketing and service provide some of the most exciting e-business opportunities. The drive over the last decade to instil new customer relationship management (CRM) techniques has resulted in varying degrees of success in recapturing that "cornershop" environment, where the proprietor knows each regular customer by name and anticipates their needs.

Much of this activity has revolved around call centres and direct mail techniques, but the internet provides a channel that can be much more personal and convenient, as well as a good deal more powerful and intelligent in the services that can be delivered. People visiting web sites can be presented with both information they have personally selected and information that the site owner has deduced they may like, based on their profile and the parts of the site they visit.

Ultimately, it is the successful marriage of customer-facing technology such as an intelligent web site with a company's customer-focused culture that will provide the most effective e-business. A company that has successfully integrated the two can present customers with an holistic view of all its relevant activities. So, for example, the customer will use a single point of entry to check on goods' shipping status, invoicing and service, whether this be a web site or by talking to a call centre agent.

Being passed from one department to another should become a distant memory for today's customer. In the future a company will not only need to "know" its customers, but to enable customers to "know" it via a transparent line of communication. This route to the company could be by new mobile smartphone technology, or by new types of device such as internet kiosks installed in retail outlets. There may be no human involvement whatsoever, since analysts are talking confidently about an age when a humble household appliance such as a washing machine will report faults and book its own service over the internet.

Meanwhile, a report researched for IT supplier Novell by the London School of Economics and E-Audits, a UK-based internet research company, has found that the world's largest, best-established "bricks and mortar" organisations have proved themselves to be better at applying themselves to e-business than smaller, emerging companies.

The *Web 2000 Top 100 Growth Report* says that large companies have more sophisticated and innovative e-business capabilities than smaller ones when it comes to the core e-commerce criteria of online ordering and payment. Having the necessary human and financial resources are the crucial factors – large e-business projects are prodigious consumers of IT infrastructure and expertise.

The researchers also found that there was no direct link between corporate growth and internet investment, suggesting that if companies invest in web technology without integrating these investments into their overall business strategy they may simply be wasting their money.

FOUR-YEAR FORECAST

It is, of course, very early days in the new wired world. But analyst firm Gartner Group is projecting worldwide business-to-business e-commerce revenues of more than $7tn by 2004, which it says will be about seven per cent of total global sales transactions. The savings that companies will make by installing new online procurement systems, for example, should start to impact significantly on the bottom-line by then. This in turn will free up capital for other activities.

Back at lastminute.com, meanwhile, a test visit resulted in a "server busy" error message – admittedly on a Friday afternoon. A new business model is only as good as the supporting infrastructure, and to that extent nothing much has changed.

DAVID AND GOLIATH

Tradepoint is an order-driven UK equity market with a difference. A virtual exchange, independent of physical location or time-zone, it opens up new possibilities in trading without incurring the costs of professional intermediation, and has a guaranteed clearing system

The exchange, which is aimed at market makers, brokers and fund managers who do not have access to the London Stock Exchange, was set up by a small group of former LSE traders committed to lowering the cost of trading in UK stocks and shares.

"It was the same as when Virgin decided to challenge BA, or Mercury took on BT. There was nothing in the law that said we couldn't do it even though historically, there was a monopoly," says Steven Wilson, Tradepoint's Marketing Manager.

"The users of our system benefit from a reduced cost, and we're offering choice where there was none before." It can also be accessed from anywhere in the world and the investor has total anonymity from order entry to settlement.

However, taking on the world's biggest stock exchange wasn't without its problems. It took the company four years to deal with the legal issues and get through the regulatory process.

There was also a lot of resistance to new methods and technology at first. The only way to beat it was by continually bringing home to people the benefits of choice and reduced cost. "We had to spend a lot of time with people trying to convince them to change their habits, but we never gave up," says Wilson.

Chapter 9

Patenting your intellectual property

The creativity and knowledge owned by a company are what distinguishes it from its competitors. IP law protects innovation and, used properly, can be a powerful tool to safeguard intellectual capital and protect business profits, says Brian Caswell, head of marketing at The Patent Office

Trevor Baylis and James Dyson have become household names in the UK and around the globe. Their success is the result of a combination of their innovation and ability to recognise a gap in the market for a new product or an application for new technology. Baylis and Dyson are representative of those inventors who have become successful and wealthy businessmen through licensing agreements or building their own companies.

Intellectual property law covers a range of legal rights which are used by companies to ensure that an invention, a technology, "look" or brand name cannot be used without the owner's permission. IP rights can be bought, sold, licensed or leased, charged or mortgaged – all of which generate revenue.

The government's Competitiveness White Paper highlighted the fundamental importance of intellectual property rights to an innovative economy. These rights are designed to address the demands of the knowledge-driven economy, and give businesses and individuals confidence to exploit their ideas commercially and undertake further innovation.

Using the intellectual property system effectively and patents in particular to protect innovation is the first step in getting the most out of an invention or new technology.

A patent is a pact between an inventor or company and the state. The state grants the applicant the right to prevent anyone from copying their invention for up to 20 years and makes public the details of the application 18 months after it is filed. In 1999 The Patent Office reported that 28,619 patent applications had been made to the UK Office, the highest number in a decade.

The system helps to spread information and knowledge from research and development programmes by making it public and, at the same time, offering protection to the companies and individuals who have invested heavily in development programmes. In some fields such as the pharmaceutical industry, research and development would be stifled without the patent system.

SECRETS OF SUCCESS

Following a few simple rules will ensure you make the most of the patent system. To get a patent, an invention must not have been published or used anywhere in the world before the application is made. Confidentiality is everything. Take the example of Coca-Cola. The drink's ingredients are a well-guarded trade secret and, despite many attempts, cannot be ascertained by analysis of the end product. The formulation of Coca-Cola has remained secret for more than a century, showing the potential longevity of properly treated confidential information.

It is impossible to patent an invention if knowledge of it already exists in the public domain. Inventors or companies with innovative new ideas and products should never make the details of their invention known before they submit a patent application.

In broad terms, an invention must fulfil the following criteria in order to get a patent. It must:

- *Be new;*

- *Not be obvious in the light of what has been done before; and*

- *Have a practical application.*

Before submitting an application, it is essential to find out what has been done in the same area. There are two reasons for this. The first is that the application will only succeed if the invention really is new. The second is that an invention may infringe someone else's patent. This is because many inventions are improvements on a prior invention. If the prior invention is less than 20 years old, it may still be protected by an existing patent. In this case, the applicant may need to come to a licensing agreement with the holder of the prior patent before licensing the invention to be manufactured, manufacturing it or selling it.

SERVICE THAT SAVES MONEY

Since 1986 The Patent Office has run the Search & Advisory Service to help inventors discover whether an invention has already been patented, or if it builds on one or more patents already in existence. But industry is still not making sufficient use of the business and technical information in the many millions of existing published patents. While The Patent Office estimates that the Search & Advisory Service saves industry at least £20m a year helping companies to solve technical problems without resorting to costly research, it also calculates that £22.5bn every year is wasted in duplicated research in Europe alone.

Eighty per cent of the technical information found in patents is not published anywhere else. There is no point reinventing the wheel. The Patent Office advises anyone who believes they have come up with a new concept or idea to get the Search & Advisory Service to check existing patents for you before embarking on costly research.

The Patent Office also advises companies and innovators to take professional advice when making a patent application, as there are many potential pitfalls and it is easy to go wrong. Patent agents specialise in framing a patent application in the right legal and technical language. Under the Register of Patent Agent Rules, the Patent Office keeps a register of those who are suitably qualified by examination and experience to call themselves patent agents.

A United Kingdom patent only grants the intellectual property rights within the UK. To stop someone making use of their invention abroad, inventors need to take out patents in the appropriate countries. The European single market does not override national patent systems so the borders are still there for patented inventions. The European Patent Office runs a system where applications are processed centrally. Patents can be granted in up to 17 European countries, including all the EU member states.

Companies that operate in the global market need to obtain wider protection. Where a new innovation has global potential and its creators are looking for patent protection in, for example, North America, South East Asia and Europe, the best approach may be to make a Patent Co-operation Treaty (PCT) application to The Patent Office in the UK. All the early processing is then made in a single application in a single language, offering considerable savings in application, patent attorney and translation fees. This method provides at least 20 months of product development and market research time in which the company or inventor can decide which countries to include.

KEEP ON THE CASE

Having secured a patent, it is up to the owner to police it and any licensing arrangements he or she may make. Intellectual property rights are business assets with the potential to make the companies or individuals who own them very wealthy. Like any other item of valuable commercial property, they must be defended. Nobody else will blow the whistle on wilful infringers and it is up to the owners of the intellectual property rights to take legal action to defend their property.

Where a patent or patents protect a valuable innovation that has the potential for widespread application, they are worth defending in court against infringement. However, the commercial value of the patent usually determines whether it is worth defending, with the costs of a court case being proportionate to the potential value of the patent. Patents with no intrinsic value are unlikely to be infringed as there is little commercial benefit in doing so, but new products with the potential to sell in global markets have greater value and are more likely to be challenged by others who recognise the potential of the idea.

Legal Aid is not available for patent infringement cases. However, patent owners can take out insurance to cover the possible costs of litigation. The decision to take out patent insurance should be made according to potential commercial value.

LITIGATION VS LICENSING

The Patent Office recommends that companies try to avoid litigation, which has a habit of being expensive as well as being critically distracting for the litigant. Where inventions are being used without authority, patent owners often seek to make a licence agreement so that the licensee pays for the use of the invention. This option allows both parties to win. The other could result in both losing.

Taking out and policing successful patents is not cheap, but the rewards can be enormous. Ask any successful inventor. For an innovative company, patent activity is not something extraneous. It must lie at the heart of any business plan, with anticipated costs and returns realistically entered.

HIGH PRICE TO PAY

When Primal Pictures conceived of a way to overcome the limitations of existing books on surgery, they knew they had to act fast to be first. But in order to fund the venture, the company gave away a substantial amount of its intellectual property

The Interactive Hand, which grew out of an academic project in collaboration with University College London (UCL), is a complete 3D digital reconstruction of the hand and forearm, from skin to bone. This gives surgeons a better understanding of the anatomy of a hand, and all serves as a useful tool to demonstrate the problem and proposed operative procedure to patients during consultations.

However, the project was hampered when the company found it difficult to secure sufficient money to do the research and earn money from the product as quickly as it needed. "We sold to a US publisher to commission the project from us," explains Laurie Wiseman, Primal Pictures' managing director. "We became 'work for hire', giving away a lot of our intellectual property. But after two years we sold part of the company and secured a grant from the the DTI. This enabled us to regain control of our own innovations and to publish ourselves."

Chapter 10

Is innovation a risky business?

For a company to be innovative, it has to embrace risk. But, says John Eggleston, national head of KPMG's owner-managed business team, risk must be managed in the right way, so as to create commercial success without jeopardising the business

Today's outstanding businesses have one common characteristic – the ability to be innovative in everything they do. Whether in strategy, product design or style of management, they appear to have an innate ability to harness innovation to achieve phenomenal success.

The entrepreneurs behind these companies have unlocked the true potential of the business, but not without a heavy dose of risk. They also understand that mismanaged or unmanaged innovation can have a devastating effect, jeopardising the very foundations of the company. The key to damage limitation lies in applying innovation to meet the demands of the business, channelling creativity in a focused way and putting in processes that give stability – a solid infrastructure unleashes the power of innovation.

EMBRACING RISK
Commercial success for any innovative business means facing head-on issues of funding, managing resources and IT. It also means addressing new challenges and pressures, including changing work patterns, intellectual property rights and protecting investment. All of these issues contain elements of risk.

The road to managing the risk of innovation within any business involves keeping abreast of all risk management issues inside and outside the organisation. Processes must be embedded which will enable management to operate effectively.

The process starts with identifying exactly what risks the business faces and how these are currently managed. These then need to be addressed in order of priority. The management team must take a controlled approach, as inevitably priorities will change as the process moves forward.

This process of embracing and prioritising risks must happen before embarking on any new project that will impact on the way the business currently operates. That way the management team will be able to understand fully existing practices within the context of the proposed changes. In short, a company needs to take the following steps to monitor and manage risk effectively:

■ *Identify and prioritise internal and external risk. Review continually;*

■ *Identify who will take responsibility for responding to risks and potential issues that arise;*

■ *Have an efficient system of internal control.*

SECURING FUNDING

Funding an innovative idea can be costly, especially in the short term when investment is high and payback from sales is not likely to materialise until the longer term. Not only does the business have to fund the development of a new product or service, it may also have to invest in materials, new manufacturing equipment, new staff, market testing, IT systems and training.

Looking for ways to release capital from within the company is a good starting point. Most business owners run a tight ship and may be doubtful about being able to identify additional revenue streams within the business. Nonetheless, a review of processes can reveal a way of releasing funds from inside the current operations. It may be that the original organisational structure has not evolved with the business and its processes. In this situation, realignment can generate significant savings that can be channelled into a new project or venture.

Another option is to use e-procurement as a means of making

cost savings. More and more businesses are seeing that purchasing through the internet can streamline the business and, consequently, release capital for other ventures.

EXTERNAL FUNDING

Innovation often occurs as a response to rapidly changing market conditions. And, as new markets are inherently riskier than established ones, shareholders expect a higher return.

If funding the development of an idea from within the business is not possible, it can be difficult to persuade outsiders to back the venture. Backing a completely new product or service that has no track record carries a far higher risk than putting money into something which has been a commercial success before and is almost guaranteed to return capital to a lender, plus interest.

There are specialist UK venture capital firms – for example, in the hi-tech sector – that will inject capital into the right innovative business. However, venture capitalists, or indeed any external funder, will be more inclined to back an innovative idea if risk has been minimised by the business. This can be achieved by carrying out some simple checks, implementing sound plans and ensuring the management team is focused.

Companies seeking external funding should ensure they can fulfil the following criteria:

- *Have a sound business plan, with realistic short, medium and long-term goals;*

- *Run a series of profit and cash projections for various "what if" scenarios to determine potential threats to cashflow;*

- *Carry out appropriate market testing;*

- *Have a good management team – 92 per cent of fund managers rate the quality of the management team as key in deciding whether or not to invest;*

- *For dot.com businesses, projections can be key. Assess impact now and in two years' time.*

Finally, don't forget that the existing assets in the business are already valuable. For example, debtors, stocks, the value of existing patents and other intellectual capital can all be used as security. It should not be necessary to give personal guarantees.

INVESTMENT IN DESIGN RESOURCES AND IP

Never forget that ownership of an innovative idea or product is a valuable asset. Innovative companies must always be mindful of the risk involved, and the potential loss, if they fail to protect their ideas in the right way. Funding innovation must embrace not only the cost involved in improving strategy and design resource for the development of a new product or service, but also the protection of that investment. With the average European patent costing around £30,000, this is not something to be overlooked. If the product or service is suitable for the international marketplace this poses additional cost implications. Think about how to co-ordinate this and who will act on the company's behalf.

IT AND E-ACTIVITIES

Developments in technology present perhaps one of the greatest risks to today's business owners. Further developments in IT will enable businesses to operate more efficiently, with associated cost benefits. However, keeping up with this fast-paced environment can be costly for any business, not only in terms of investing in kit, but those organisations which do not take advantage and develop will become the business failures of the future.

In particular, e-commerce is already having a massive impact, opening up global markets and driving down costs. Customers will continue to become increasingly sophisticated as through technology they access a wealth of information to facilitate comparison of prices and products.

E-commerce also releases the potential of new and innovative ideas. Does this mean businesses need to re-think business strategy and come up with a new plan to show how e-commerce will add value to the business? Or does it simply mean adapting business processes to cater for e-commerce? No matter how e-commerce impacts on a business, in most cases it will bring about some element of change, prompting the need for risk assessment and possibly an injection of cash – whether it be from a specialist venture capitalist or an incubator funding programme. At the very least, companies need to:

- *Assess the impact of e-business on your company – now;*

- *If e-commerce is driving innovation in your business, think how this is going to be funded.*

HEAVEN SENT

Unable to pursue their ideas in a large company, the developers of SoftCDTM set up their own, iOra Limited, to create a software product that allows companies to distribute remote information and keep it up to date quickly, cost-effectively and securely

While traditional CD-ROMs have the capacity for huge multimedia and software programmes, they cannot be updated and soon become out of date. Meanwhile, the internet is continuously being updated, but is too slow to handle multimedia applications. SoftCDTM offers the best of both worlds, updating CDs via a website by creating an "electronic erratum".

The company gathered feedback about the product's potential by inviting both multimedia services and potential corporate customers to seminars. "Until we were able to demonstrate that the product could work, people wouldn't believe us," explains Paddy Falls, iOra's managing director.

Initially the founders invested their own money, but secured £300,000 of investment from a group of four Business Angels at the prototype stage. The Business Angels had previously been senior executives at Dell, Apple and QA Training in the UK. Then in June 99, it obtained a further £2m of investment capital from UK venture capital company MTI Partners after demonstrating that it could build the product and having made some early sales.

"Having the secure funding and advice from the Business Angels, and having a close-knit team that was experienced and motivated were the key factors in our successfully developing the product," says Falls.

"The venture capital investment has also been critical in allowing us to build a sales and marketing team and implement the scale of marketing programs that will enable much greater revenue growth."

Chapter 11

Sustainable development

Innovation in manufacturing and process technology is vital if sustainable development is to be achieved in the new millennium. Ron Biagioni, engineering and manufacturing director, 3M United Kingdom, highlights the issues in this key area

3M is perhaps best known for the popular Post-it Note. What is less well-known is the scale and diversity of its operations. The company develops and sells over 50,000 products to a vast range of markets, from aerospace to health care, from the office to the home. These innovations are the result of the commercial exploitation of 30 core technology platforms together with the imagination of our scientists, technicians and engineers who are encouraged to develop the groundbreaking products of the future.

The far-reaching nature of 3M's business creates environmental challenges too. The company uses large quantities of energy and materials, and it generates waste. But it is committed to embracing a new way of doing business – in which it creates shareholder value and builds a better quality of life and a more sustainable future.

Following the 1992 Rio Earth Summit, industry leaders from around the world have paid increasing attention to the environmental impacts of their activities. They also realise that the smart companies of the future will be the ones that create competitive advantage out of good environmental practice.

Understanding the business value to be gained from greater "eco-efficiency" is an important first step towards sustainable development, and has been well documented. The introduction of a new lightweight PET blister pack for a SmithKline Beecham toothbrush reduced material consumption per pack by 70 per cent.

The energy saving alone of 116 million megajoules was the equivalent of the energy required to light every US home for one hour. Energy efficiency, waste minimisation, lower costs and improved employee morale are all good for business.

But today's customers want more than just new products and believe business, like government, should be accountable for its actions. As such, business should not only think about the bottom line but also play an active role in managing the world's resources to meet the needs of future generations.

WHAT DOES SUSTAINABLE DEVELOPMENT MEAN?

Sustainable development is a very simple idea. It means meeting the needs of customers today while respecting the ability of future generations to meet their needs.

While 3M has always paid close attention to the environment, our business is moving toward sustainable development systematically. The environmental effect of our activities is considered at every step in our business.

Within this context, we have developed a formal environmental policy that spans almost three decades. We were one of the first companies to make our responsibility for the environment part of company practice, in 1975. Our environmental policy calls on 3M to solve its own environmental problems and meet, or preferably exceed, government regulations. It also focuses on preventing pollution, conserving natural resources and developing products that have minimum effect on the environment.

Motivated by a desire to protect the environment for future generations, 3M employees have eliminated more than 540,000 metric tonnes of pollution to air, land and water and significantly cut pollution per unit of production.

Preventing pollution at its source was not a new idea, but applying it on a permanent and worldwide basis was. The achievements of our 3P programme (Pollution Prevention Pays) are testimony to the topline support from management and the dedication and involvement by all our employees. In its first 20 years, 3M staff originated 4,450 projects, through the tried and tested route of identifying new opportunities for innovation. Typically, innovation takes the form of:

■ *Product reformulation;*

■ *Process modification;*

■ *Equipment redesign;*

■ *Recycling and re-use of raw materials.*

The environment is an integral part of the way we do business and innovation fuels our growth. 3M devotes a proportion of its $1bn-plus annual research and development budget to reducing the environmental impact of new and existing products and to improving manufacturing processes. This has led to improvements or new developments for more than 100 products.

One technology platform, Microreplication, uses a solventless manufacturing process and involves making precise, microscopic changes to the surface of different materials to influence their performance. Another example is a brightness enhancement film for laptop computer screens. This consists of millions of tiny, optically perfect lenses embossed onto the surface of a clear plastic film to provide a brighter computer screen. The environmental advantage comes from smaller batteries that draw less power, last longer, and reduce disposal costs.

STRETCH GOALS

Like many companies, 3M believes that external scrutiny of our systems will lead to improved reliability and awareness. Our environmental management systems (EMS) incorporate environmental best practice, our business strategy and compliance with legislation. This year, all 3M sites worldwide will have received certification to at least ISO 9002 and across all 25 manufacturing plants Europe will have ISO14001 by the end of 2000.

Eventually 3M intends to cut waste and environmental releases to as close to zero as possible. These goals are set to bring about systematic rather than incremental changes.

Innovation will continue to make our environmental task easier. For example, a hot-melt process that took nine years to develop has resulted in substantial benefits. At one manufacturing plant alone, the process eliminated 1,100 metric tonnes of solvent per year and reduced energy consumption by 77 per cent. It also reduced manufacturing cycle time by 25 per cent.

MOVING BEYOND COMPLIANCE

For the future, environmental performance at 3M will require a greater focus on the entire life cycle of products, from development and manufacturing through to customer use and disposal. This will involve closer interaction with suppliers and customers to manage continuous environmental improvements.

3M Pharmaceuticals recently used this approach to develop the world's first CFC-free metered dose inhaler (MDI) for the treatment of asthma. Granted Millennium Product status by the Design Council, the Qvar inhaler required far more than just the exchange of one propellant for another. Every component of the MDI system, as well as the manufacturing and quality assurance processes, was reassessed and in many cases, redesigned. The inhaler dispenses an entirely new formulation of extra fine particles to improve the delivery of the medicine to the lungs and offers asthma patients the opportunity to at least halve doses of inhaled steroids compared with the CFC products it replaces.

CONCLUSION

The Rio Earth Summit pressed companies to pay closer attention to the environmental impact of their activities. Big companies, after all, are major players in today's global economy and can influence a change towards more sustainable production and consumption.

Business, however, does not operate in isolation and cannot solve the world's problems alone. Closer interaction and co-operation between business, government and society is required if we are to create value for a company and civilisation by doing more with less. Organisations such as the Centre for Tomorrow's Company, the Prince of Wales Business Leaders' Forum and the

Business for Social Responsibility (USA) have emerged in recent years to raise awareness of environmental and corporate responsibility issues and promote best practice among businesses.

The World Business Council for Sustainable Development (WBCSD) now has over 120 individual members across 34 countries and from more than 20 major industrial sectors. This is further evidence that business is keen to progress toward sustainable development. Nevertheless, much more work needs to be done.

Today's successful companies are those that manage change and maximise their greatest resource – the talents of a capable and committed workforce. Tomorrow's winners will be companies that create financial wealth for their shareholders within an operation of clearly defined principles and values. This code of conduct would include levels of social and environmental responsibility so far disregarded by many companies. Finding the balance will be the task we all face in this century. The companies that fail may simply disappear.

Sources

Eco-efficiency: The Business Link to Sustainable Development
Livio D DeSimone and Frank Popoff (1997)

Corporate Citizenship
McIntosh, Leipziger, Jones and Coleman (1998)

Chapter 12

New horizons

What will be the global macroeconomic and social effects of rapid technological innovation? Peter Cochrane, chief technologist at BT and Collier Chair for The Public Understanding of Science & Technology at Bristol University, looks at the big picture, consults his crystal ball and poses some provocative thoughts

Predicting future trends is a dangerous pastime but, to start on a positive note, two magical realisations look set to nudge the economic climate of the UK in the right direction.

The first, and probably the most important, is the growing acceptance by society that making money and becoming wealthy is now more or less OK, and it might even turn out to be good.

The second, which is both a relief and perhaps our saviour in the long term, is the growing recognition that being online is advantageous. It has been some time coming, but at last we seem to have grasped the realisation that without wealth generation we can do nothing to achieve our desired social goals, and if we are not online we will be out of the race to create wealth.

But there is another realisation yet to come: the ability to accept and respond to continual change as the absolute essential for a vibrant economy. To slightly misquote Charles Darwin: "It is not the strongest or smartest who survive, but those most adaptable to change". The last time this was considered significant was during the Victorian era when the telephone started to transform our ability to communicate and organise.

In most industries there has been a stark realisation that globalisation means tough competition and a fight for survival. But unlike any previous period in our history, businesses face a world that is becoming increasingly fast, counter-intuitive and commercially more dangerous. Consider, for example, the polarised perception of e-commerce in the US and Europe, exemplified by recent events in the entertainment industry. European headlines and reports recently read along the lines: "Time Warner buys AOL" and within a week it became, "Time Warner buys AOL and EMI". This was followed by reports expressing some sense of relief that real bricks-and-mortar money had overcome the unreal and inflated world of internet stocks. Meanwhile, on the other side of the Atlantic, the headline was: "AOL buys Time Warner and EMI" followed by reports that unreal money does it again.

NEW MEASURES OF VALUE

It seems that value is actually perception. But are today's investments in the dot.com world any less credulous and long-lasting than the purchase of an Old Master – just paint on canvas with no intrinsic value? Or antique furniture – just a few sticks of wood. Here we have items fundamentally worth nothing that are valued in millions of pounds or dollars.

By comparison, the dot.com world looks more solidly founded, with customers, a service base, knowledge and a growing influence over the lives of everyone on the planet. The only uncertainty hinges on their real value, and that comes down to what people are prepared to spend, which we generally count in financial terms. A wiser choice of metric may turn out to be time. The key to calculating the value of a dot.com business may be how many people are attracted to a web site or service, and how much time they are prepared to devote to it.

Richard Feynman, one of the greatest physicists that ever lived, once said: "I think we can safely assume that no one understands quantum mechanics". This is probably even more likely to be correct today. Unfortunately there has never been a Richard Feynman of economics, or indeed any theories that come remotely close to explaining what is happening within markets. Nevertheless: "I think we can safely assume that no one understands the internet and the dot.com world".

The dynamic nature of relationships and the involvement of human emotions, creativity and greed result in a high level of unpredictability. But if a Feynman of economic theory does turn up, I suspect the key formulae for value will include knowledge, information, access, reach, relationships, time, products and customer base as wholly stronger parameters than raw money.

BLIND TO THE THREAT

If we could understand all of this it would be easier to predict the future. But just looking at dot.com stocks and their rate of growth – where companies are amassing billions in less than five years – it is clear that many of today's bricks-and-mortar megaliths face the risk of being bought out within the next 18 months. Banks, insurance companies, telcos and cable companies are all threatened, but I'm not at all sure many of them see it coming.

I watch with interest as the technologically celibate pontificate on the pros and cons, the opportunities and dangers of information technology they have never experienced. The innovation of the internet and its enthusiastic embrace by the US seems merely to promote one talking shop after another in Europe, where the predominant focus seems to be on the abuse of IT and the internet rather than the commercial or social advantages they offer.

THE BIG PICTURE

As far as I can see, the next big deal has to be the notion of zero government involvement and intervention in trade. Two states in the US are actively considering a total move out of control and regulation on all forms of trade.

Could this be the end game? After all, we started with total freedom and migrated through dictatorship, communism, and capitalism in cycles that now see capitalism the current victor. In fact, the only system to create most change and benefit in terms of standard of living and basic freedoms has been capitalism. But is it sustainable in the grand context of the use of raw materials and preserving the ecosystem of the planet? I think not. Rampant commercialism will ultimately fell all the trees, burn all the oil and coal, and gradually destroy the environment to a level where we cannot survive.

The rise in the number of cancer cases, allergies, overcrowded cities, and the possibility that we have triggered global warming are but a few issues already evident.

So how could total freedom work? Will it not be even more damaging to the planet than capitalism or communism? Broadly, we are seeing commercial focus gradually moving from the industrial economy to the electronic economy (or e.conomy) to be followed by the corporate conscience and the ECOnomy.

Ultimately, this could result in a freedom of trade and action that borders on anarchy, but in a constructive and dynamic manner that may realise the maximum benefit to society and the players. What is surprising is the length of time it has taken for governments to recognise that they not only have no role, but that they are now the most likely impediment to progress.

IT not only changes the speed and manner in which we can trade and do business but, more radically, it changes the fundamental characteristics of modern societies.

BACK TO BUSINESS

The population concerned with start-up businesses is around three per cent in the UK, five per cent in Israel, seven per cent in Canada and nine per cent in the US. In each case, about 30 per cent of new economic growth is generated by start-ups, and most of those involved are under 45 years old.

The UK resides in the lower quartile of the league table with a discouraging tax system and an inadequate infrastructure that fails to promote the exploitation of our primary wealth generator – ideas. It is difficult even to rent floor space by the day or week, and support services are expensive.

Today we have a scattering of start-ups operating at a subsistence level and nothing remotely approaching the US model where incubators are being developed on a massive scale. Unfortunately we seem to have few people who recognise the need to drive this forward, and there is still resistance to the idea that taking risks deserves greater reward – and that to try and fail is preferable to never trying at all.

Nonetheless, this culture is changing, but slowly. As a matter of economic survival we have to fix all of this fast to ensure our future prosperity.

FOSTERING INNOVATION

So what can be done to realise a magical transformation of industry and business? This shortlist of actions should ensure future success:

■ *Keep it simple. Create a clear and easily understandable vision; evangelise and sell to all the players and people involved – communication is always the vital element.*

■ *Under-manage. Let go at the top, empower people to succeed and provide the framework in which everyone is a partner.*

■ *Seek out supportive relationships. Find organisations, companies and people who salute and support your cause, and with the skills and facilities to satisfy and supply your needs – it is easier to be a winner when working with winners.*

■ *Build networks early. All forms of networks bring high returns.*

■ *Invert the rules. The value chain of the new is unlikely to resemble the old and will almost certainly be inverted.*

■ *Seek exponential growth. Find the routes to and mechanisms for explosive growth that far exceeds the old linear markets.*

■ *Focus on customers. The future of business is about sucking up - really sucking up!*

■ *Virtualise. Outsource as much as possible - the days of Do It All have long gone.*

■ *Technologise. Use the best available - ultimately it costs far less than people - and you cannot win against competition with superior fire power.*

■ *Make information free. Let people have access - for without communication and data availability they will be disabled and ineffective.*

■ *Reward everyone. Make sure that all involved get a significant slice of any success.*

■ *Celebrate the winners and care for those in trouble. Remember the power of praise and the rehabilitating impact of concern and support.*

A TARGET TO AIM FOR

Consider a Fortune 500 company that didn't exist 15 years ago. It manages the expenses for over 20,000 staff with only two people. Everyone is trusted and electronic screening, with a few spot checks on reports lying outside the norm, is all that is required to police the system. Now consider the governmental or "old company" approach – no-one is trusted and hundreds are employed to watch and police the activities of the rest. The cost is huge and the benefits negligible. People feel untrusted and unloved, while those wishing to defraud the company do it anyway and largely escape because it is unrealistic to devote sufficient resources to detecting and tracking crimes.

IT, the internet, and freedom really work – but it is more about changing mindsets and behaviour than technology.